SUPER FOOTBALL INFOGRAPHICS

Eric Braun

graphics by
Laura Westlund

Lerner Publications • Minneapolis

Lerner Publications Company
A division of Lerner Publishing Group, Inc.
241 First Avenue North
Minneapolis, MN USA 55401

For reading levels and more information, look up this title at www.lernerbooks.com.

Main text set in Univers LT Std 12/15.
Typeface provided by Adobe Systems.

Library of Congress Cataloging-in-Publication Data

Braun, Eric, 1971–
        Super football infographics / by Eric Braun.
            pages   cm. — (Super sports infographics)
        Includes index.
        Audience: Age: 8–11.
        ISBN 978-1-4677-5231-2 (lib. bdg. : alk. paper)
        ISBN 978-1-4677-7576-2 (pbk.)
        ISBN 978-1-4677-6277-9 (EB pdf)
        1. Football–Graphic methods–Juvenile literature. I. Title.
    GV950.7.B73 2015
    796.332021—dc23   2014010986

Manufactured in the United States of America
1 – DP – 12/31/14

CONTENTS

HUT, HUT, HIKE!

Football in fall is as traditional as mustard on a hot dog. Take this quick quiz to see how big a fan you are:

1. Do you love to spend Sunday afternoons watching the National Football League (NFL) on TV?

2. Have you ever huddled with friends on the playground drawing up a play in the dirt?

3. Do you know who the highest-paid player in the NFL is?

4. Are you curious about who kicked the longest field goal in NFL history?

Did you answer yes to any of those questions?

THEN IT'S TIME FOR KICKOFF!

You're ready to dig deeper into this thrilling game. From kids on playgrounds to pros on the gridiron, football is full of action. Anything can happen once the ball is snapped. Long bombs, power runs, fumbles, trick plays, and more—football has excitement to spare.

Whether you love to play or prefer to watch, charts, graphs, and other infographics can help you learn more about football. So hike the ball and go long!

SUPER BOWL
CHAMPIONS

GETTING SCHOOLED

The NFL doesn't have minor leagues like other sports. Instead, players master the game at the college level. Each spring, the 32 NFL teams take turns choosing college players in the NFL draft.

Some universities are excellent at developing their football players. But which school has bragging rights for training the most NFL players? That can change from year to year. NFL careers are often short, and team rosters tend to be very different from one year to the next. Here are the 12 schools that had the most former students on NFL teams in the first week of the 2013 season.

UNIVERSITY OF SOUTHERN CALIFORNIA
40

LOUISIANA STATE UNIVERSITY
39

UNIVERSITY OF MIAMI
38

UNIVERSITY OF GEORGIA
36

FLORIDA STATE UNIVERSITY
31

UNIVERSITY OF TEXAS
31

UNIVERSITY OF ALABAMA
30

UNIVERSITY OF CALIFORNIA, BERKELEY
30

UNIVERSITY OF TENNESSEE
30

OHIO STATE UNIVERSITY
27

UNIVERSITY OF OREGON
27

UNIVERSITY OF FLORIDA
26

CAREER PASSING LEADERS

The NFL has had some amazing quarterbacks in its long history. Some of those killer passers have thrown for so many yards, your arm gets sore just thinking about it.

Brett Favre is the NFL's all-time leading passer in terms of yards. He has thrown for 71,838 yards. That's about 41 miles (66 kilometers)! The widest part of the Grand Canyon is only 18 miles (29 km) across. Favre threw for enough yards to cross it and come back again, with 5 miles (8 km) to spare. Here's what Favre's passing yards look like stacked up against some other long distances.

5   10   15   20

0

Maui, the second-largest Hawaiian island   48 miles (77 km) long

Brett Favre   71,838 passing yards (41 miles, or 66 km)

Peyton Manning   64,964 passing yards (37 miles, or 60 km)*

Dan Marino   61,361 passing yards (35 miles, or 56 km)

Channel Tunnel   31 miles (50 km) from England to France

Marathon race   26.2 miles (42 km)

Grand Canyon   18 miles (29 km) across at the widest point

Manhattan Island   13 miles (21 km) long

0   21

*through the end of the 2013 season

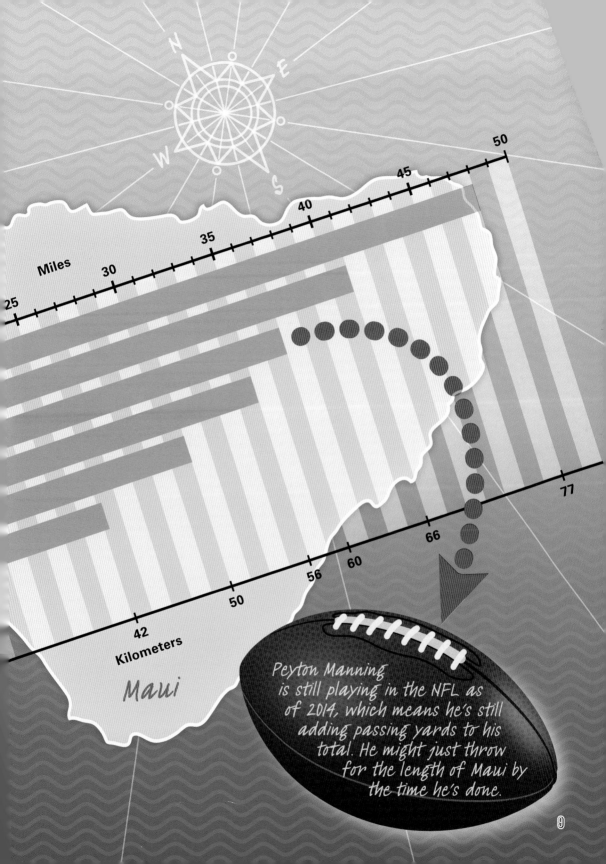

Miles

25 30 35 40 45 50

Kilometers

42 50 56 60 66 77

Maui

Peyton Manning is still playing in the NFL as of 2014, which means he's still adding passing yards to his total. He might just throw for the length of Maui by the time he's done.

WHY SPIRAL?

For a football fan, few things are as pretty as a well-thrown pass. It's easy to admire those amazing spirals floating through the air. But is there a reason other than beauty that quarterbacks try to throw spirals? Of course there is.

Once a quarterback throws a ball, two forces act on it to change its path: gravity and air. You can't do much about gravity. That ball is coming down again, no matter what. But a tight spin, or spiral, helps the ball cut through the air. The spin of the ball reduces the number of air particles that hit it, thus reducing air drag. With less air pushing on the ball, it can go straighter and farther. Compare that to a kicked ball that tumbles end over end.

The spin a quarterback puts on a ball is called torque.

A football thrown in a spiral at 60 miles (97 km) per hour is subject to about 0.2 pounds (0.09 kilograms) of air drag.

air drag

air particle

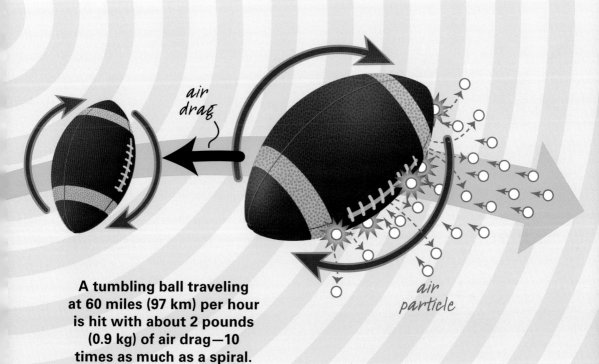

air drag

A tumbling ball traveling at 60 miles (97 km) per hour is hit with about 2 pounds (0.9 kg) of air drag—10 times as much as a spiral.

air particle

WHO'S GETTING PAID?

You probably know that pro athletes make a lot of money. And since football is so popular, NFL players are among the highest paid. But which players make the most? The salaries shown here represent the ten highest contracts by yearly average in the NFL as of September 2014.

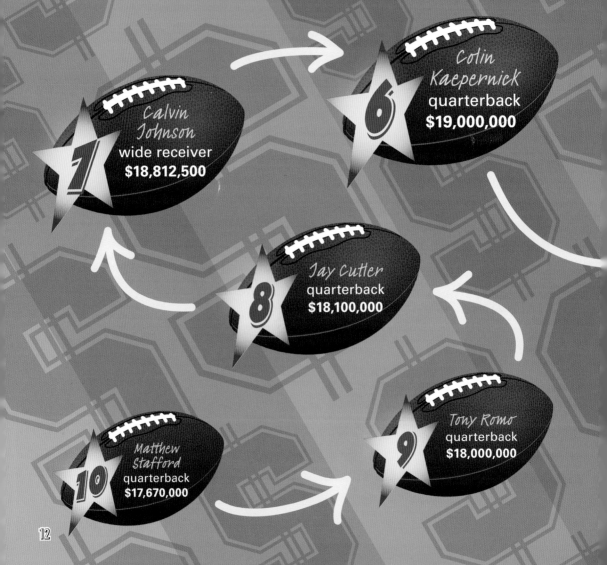

6
Colin Kaepernick
quarterback
$19,000,000

7
Calvin Johnson
wide receiver
$18,812,500

8
Jay Cutler
quarterback
$18,100,000

9
Tony Romo
quarterback
$18,000,000

10
Matthew Stafford
quarterback
$17,670,000

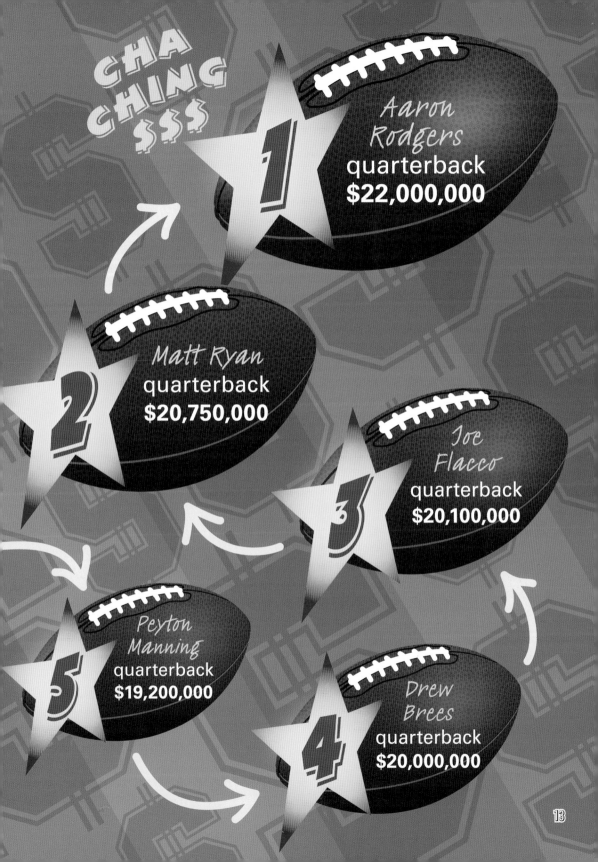

THE KICK IS UP— THE KICK IS GOOD!

Have you ever felt a little sorry for kickers? They typically put up more points than anyone else during the season, but they don't get the glory that quarterbacks and other offensive heroes receive. Fans and teammates take kickers for granted—that is, until the game is on the line.

When you *need* that long field goal to win or tie, the kicker suddenly becomes the most important player on the field. And if you think about it, kicking a funny-shaped ball a looooong distance between two poles is pretty amazing. Here are the longest field goals on record in Division I college football and the NFL.

67 YARDS

Three kickers have made field goals from this distance in college: Russel Erxleben of the University of Texas, on October 15, 1977; Steve Little of the University of Arkansas, on October 15, 1977; and Joe Williams of Wichita State University, on October 21, 1978.

64 YARDS

On December 8, 2013, Matt Prater of the Denver Broncos blasted this kick against the Tennessee Titans. It was the longest field goal in NFL history. The shoes he wore that day are in the Pro Football Hall of Fame.

63 YARDS

Four NFL kickers have drilled field goals from this distance. Tom Dempsey of the New Orleans Saints did it on November 8, 1970. Jason Elam of the Denver Broncos equaled it on October 25, 1998. Oakland Raiders kicker Sebastian Janikowski was the next to do it on September 12, 2011. Finally, David Akers of the San Francisco 49ers did it on September 9, 2012.

ANATOMY OF A HELMET

A football helmet might look simple from the outside. But it's a complicated device designed to guard the most precious part of the human body—the brain. After all, if you're repeatedly bashing your head against a 300-pound (136 kg) man at high speeds, you're going to want some serious protection.

As we've learned more about head injuries, football helmets have changed. They've gotten better at protecting players. Take a look at how helmets have evolved over the years.

Early Helmet

Early leather helmets were designed mainly to protect the ears. Helmets were made of leather on the outside and were lined with a thin layer of felt.

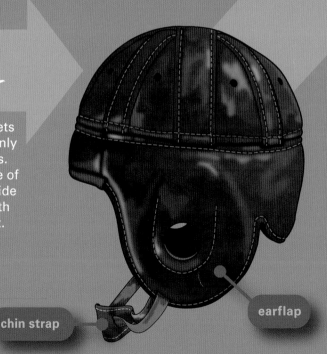

chin strap

earflap

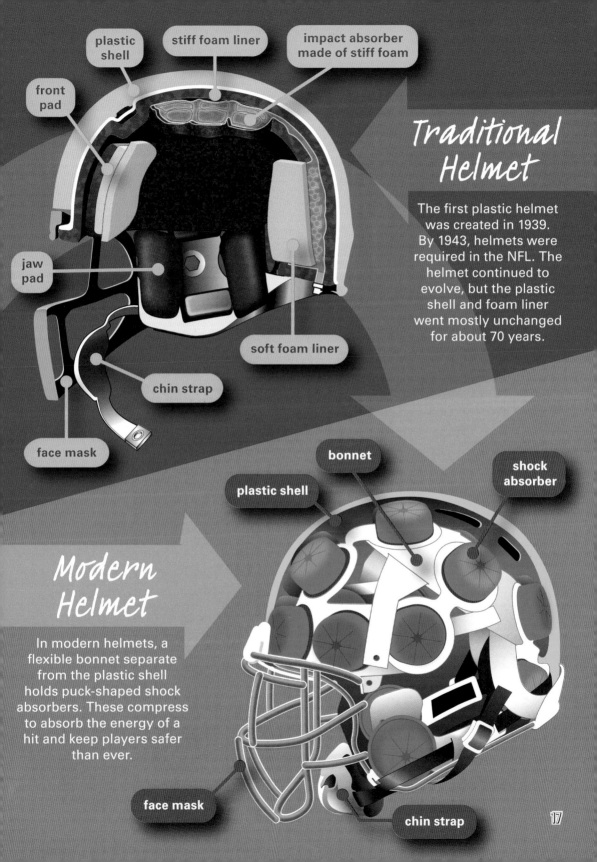

plastic
shell

stiff foam liner

impact absorber
made of stiff foam

front
pad

jaw
pad

soft foam liner

chin strap

face mask

Traditional Helmet

The first plastic helmet was created in 1939. By 1943, helmets were required in the NFL. The helmet continued to evolve, but the plastic shell and foam liner went mostly unchanged for about 70 years.

bonnet

plastic shell

shock absorber

Modern Helmet

In modern helmets, a flexible bonnet separate from the plastic shell holds puck-shaped shock absorbers. These compress to absorb the energy of a hit and keep players safer than ever.

face mask

chin strap

BIG MEN GETTING BIGGER

Pro football players are probably not good at hide-and-seek. Where do you hide if you're 6 feet 6 inches (2 meters) tall and weigh 350 pounds (159 kg)?

Football players work hard to become as big and strong as possible. But they haven't always been *this* big. In 1970, only one player in the NFL weighed as much as 300 pounds (136 kg). In 2013, more than 500 players tipped the scales at 300 pounds or more. The biggest guys on the field are usually the offensive linemen. They need to be huge to protect the quarterback and clear paths for running backs. Check out how offensive linemen of the past compare with recent years.

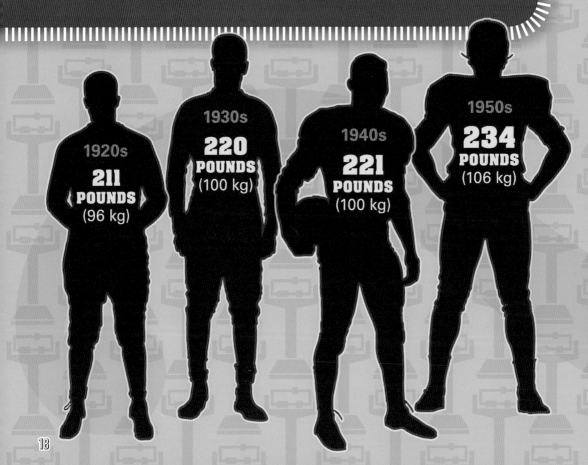

1920s
211 POUNDS (96 kg)

1930s
220 POUNDS (100 kg)

1940s
221 POUNDS (100 kg)

1950s
234 POUNDS (106 kg)

2013
310
POUNDS
(141 kg)

2000s
313
POUNDS
(142 kg)

1990s
300
POUNDS
(136 kg)

1960s
251
POUNDS
(114 kg)

1970s
255
POUNDS
(116 kg)

1980s
272
POUNDS
(123 kg)

GETTING OFFENSIVE

Passing the football in the NFL used to be a lot more risky than it is now. Blocking rules made it hard for offensive linemen to keep defenders from getting to the quarterback. Defensive backs could knock wide receivers off their routes anywhere on the field. So, fewer passes were attempted. The scoring average of all the teams in the NFL declined to an all-time low of about 17 points per game in 1977.

In 1978, the NFL began to make changes to the rules. Offensive linemen were allowed more freedom to block defenders. Defensive backs could only touch wide receivers within five yards of the line of scrimmage. These changes made it a lot easier to pass the ball. Rules put in place in recent years to protect the quarterbacks from injury have caused teams to throw the ball more and score more points than ever. On the timeline to the right, you can see how the average points scored per game in the NFL has changed since 1977.

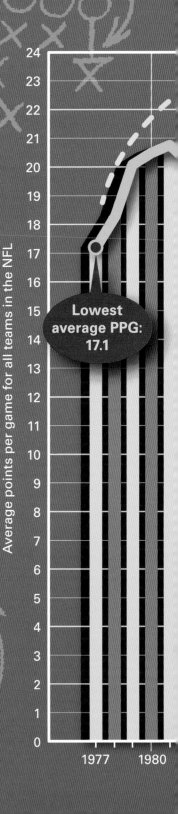

Average points per game for all teams in the NFL

24
23
22
21
20
19
18
17
16
15
14
13
12
11
10
9
8
7
6
5
4
3
2
1
0

Lowest average PPG: 17.1

1977   1980

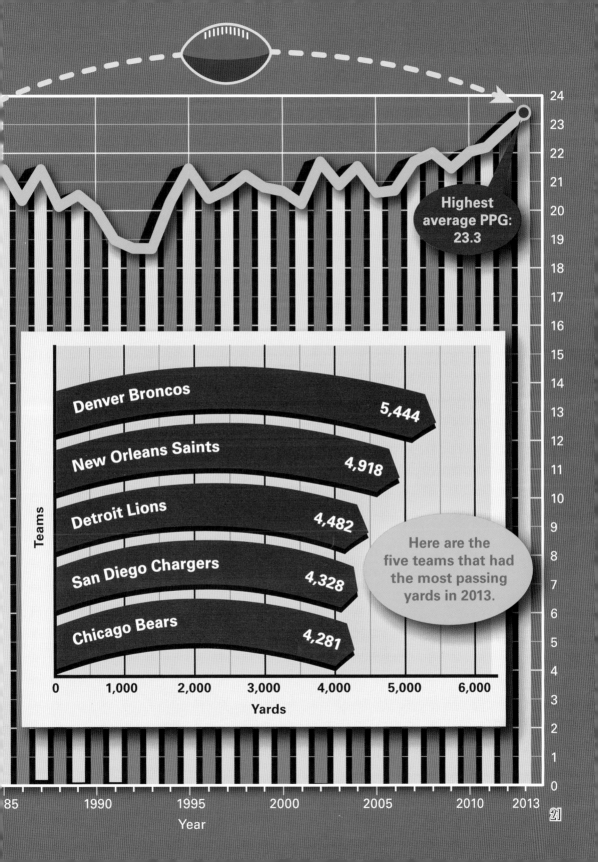

Highest average PPG: 23.3

Teams

Denver Broncos — 5,444

New Orleans Saints — 4,918

Detroit Lions — 4,482

San Diego Chargers — 4,328

Chicago Bears — 4,281

Yards

0   1,000   2,000   3,000   4,000   5,000   6,000

Here are the five teams that had the most passing yards in 2013.

85   1990   1995   2000   2005   2010   2013

Year

COLD ENOUGH FOR YA?

When the football season starts in early fall, players often wear short sleeves and pour water over their heads to stay cool. As the season goes on, temperatures drop and games are played in cold, snowy, ruthless conditions.

The coldest pro game ever played was the famous Ice Bowl, the NFL championship game of December 31, 1967. When the Dallas Cowboys and the Green Bay Packers faced off at Lambeau Field in Green Bay, Wisconsin, the temperature at kickoff was −13°F (−25°C). But the icy wind made it feel like −48° F (−44°C). Check out more of the coldest games in pro football history.

-30°C

-40°C

-30°

-40°F

-50°F

0°C

40°F

30°F

-10°C

20°F

10°F

0°F

-10°F

2°F (−17°C)
Green Bay Packers
vs. Detroit Lions in
Green Bay, Wisconsin,
December 22, 1990

0°F (−18°C) Minnesota Vikings vs. Green
Bay Packers in Bloomington, Minnesota,
December 10, 1972

0°F (−18°C) Green Bay Packers vs. Los
Angeles Raiders in Green Bay, Wisconsin,
December 26, 1993

0°F (−18°C°) Buffalo Bills vs. Los Angeles Raiders
in Buffalo, New York, January 15, 1994

−2°F (−19°C) Chicago Bears vs. Minnesota Vikings
in Bloomington, Minnesota, December 3, 1972

−4°F (−20°C) Green Bay Packers vs. New York
Giants in Green Bay, Wisconsin, January 20, 2008

−5°F (−21°C) Cleveland Browns vs. Oakland
Raiders in Cleveland, Ohio, January 4, 1981

−6°F (−21°C) Kansas City Chiefs vs. Indianapolis
Colts in Kansas City, Missouri, January 7, 1996

−9°F (−23°C) Cincinnati Bengals vs. San Diego
Chargers in Cincinnati, Ohio, January 10, 1982

−13°F (−25°C) Green Bay Packers
vs. Dallas Cowboys
in Green Bay, Wisconsin,
December 31, 1967

THE 12TH MAN

Football fans are known to be passionate and loud. When the 11 players on the field for the home team make a great play, the crowd roars. This loud support can give home teams an advantage in games, which is why the crowd is sometimes called the 12th man. It's like the home team has an extra player.

On December 2, 2013, the crowd in Seattle, Washington, roared so loudly that they literally shook the earth. They caused an earthquake of between 1.0 and 2.0 on the Richter scale. Here's how the noise the Seattle crowd made that day compares to other noises.

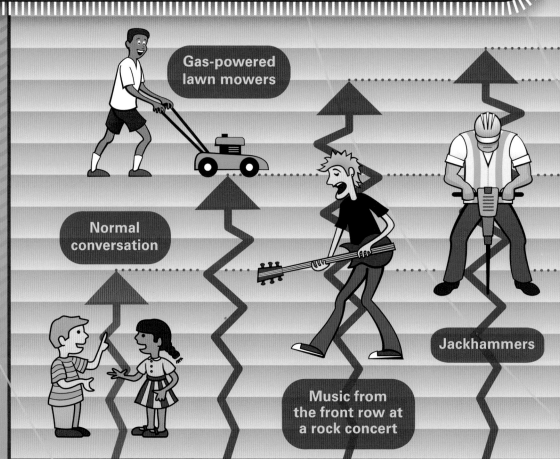

Gas-powered lawn mowers

Normal conversation

Jackhammers

Music from the front row at a rock concert

THE NFL—
NICE FINANCES LEAGUE

The business of professional football is booming, which is great news if you're a team owner. Teams are worth more money than ever as more and more fans enjoy the sport. Check out the top five most valuable NFL teams, the average value of an NFL team, and the five least valuable teams in 2013.

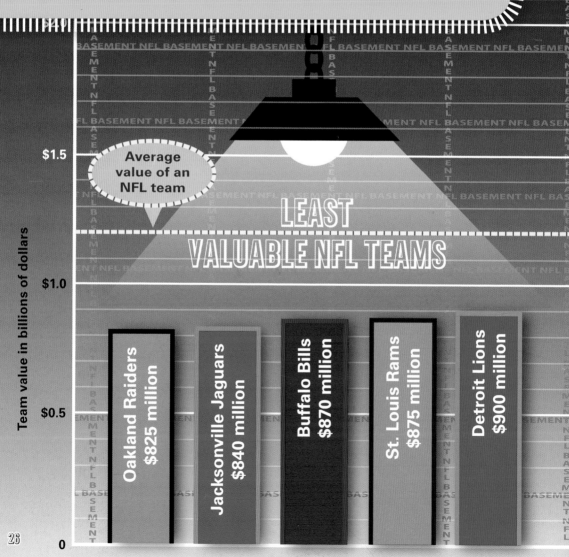

Team value in billions of dollars

$1.5

Average value of an NFL team

LEAST VALUABLE NFL TEAMS

$1.0

$0.5

Oakland Raiders $825 million

Jacksonville Jaguars $840 million

Buffalo Bills $870 million

St. Louis Rams $875 million

Detroit Lions $900 million

0

Houston Texans
$1.5 billion

Washington Redskins
$1.7 billion

Dallas Cowboys
$2.3 billion

New England Patriots
$1.8 billion

New York Giants
$1.6 billion

$2.5

$2.0

$1.5

$1.0

$0.5

0

MOST VALUABLE NFL TEAMS

SUPER SUNDAYS

The Super Bowl is a lot like a holiday. Every year, fans get together to watch, cheer, and laugh at the game and TV commercials. More people watch the Super Bowl on TV than any other show all year.

Because the Super Bowl is the biggest football game of the year, every NFL team starts the new season with the goal of winning it. But only one team per year can reach that goal. Take a look at the teams that have won the Super Bowl and the years that they did it.

SUPER BOWL CHAMPIONS

5 WINS

6 WINS

Pittsburgh Steelers: 1975, 1976, 1979, 1980, 2006, 2009

Dallas Cowboys:
1972, 1978, 1993, 1994, 1996

San Francisco 49ers:
1982, 1985, 1989, 1990, 1995

WINS 4

Green Bay Packers: 1967, 1968, 1997, 2011

New York Giants: 1987, 1991, 2008, 2012

3 WINS

Washington Redskins: 1983, 1988, 1992

New England Patriots: 2002, 2004, 2005

Oakland Raiders/ Los Angeles Raiders: 1977, 1981, 1984

Denver Broncos: 1998, 1999

Baltimore Ravens: 2001, 2013

2 WINS

Baltimore Colts/ Indianapolis Colts: 1971, 2007

Miami Dolphins: 1973, 1974

1

St. Louis Rams/ Cleveland Rams/ Los Angeles Rams: 2000

Seattle Seahawks: 2014

New Orleans Saints: 2010

Tampa Bay Buccaneers: 2003

Chicago Bears: 1986

Kansas City Chiefs: 1970

New York Jets: 1969

Glossary

AIR DRAG: also known as air resistance, this is the force that air puts on an object in motion to slow it down

BONNET: a protective device in modern football helmets that holds shock absorbers

DECIBEL: a unit for measuring sound

DEFENSIVE BACK: a defensive player whose main job is to cover wide receivers and keep them from catching passes

DIVISION I: the top level of college athletics

FELT: a fabric that is matted instead of being woven

GRIDIRON: a football field

LINE OF SCRIMMAGE: an imaginary line where each play begins

NFL DRAFT: an annual event at which NFL teams take turns choosing college players

OFFENSIVE LINEMAN: a player whose job is to protect the quarterback on pass plays and make room for the running back on running plays

RICHTER SCALE: a scale for measuring the power of an earthquake

SPIRAL: when something spins around a central point. A spiral in football is a ball thrown with a controlled spin that doesn't wobble.

TORQUE: a force that makes something rotate or spin. A quarterback puts torque on a football when he throws it.

UNIVERSITY: a school after high school where students follow a specific course of study

Further Information

ESPN
http://ESPN.go.com
This website is a huge resource for sports news, feature stories, stats, fantasy games, and more.

Fishman, Jon M. *Richard Sherman.* Minneapolis: Lerner Publications, 2015. Read all about the life of Richard Sherman and how he helped the Seattle Seahawks win the Super Bowl in 2014.

Jacobs, Greg. *The Everything KIDS' Football Book: All-Time Greats, Legendary Teams, and Today's Favorite Players—with Tips on Playing like a Pro.* 4th ed. New York: Adams Media, 2014. This all-around resource explains how the game works and provides rules, history, profiles, and football puzzles.

McClafferty, Carla Killough. *Fourth Down and Inches: Concussions and Football's Make-or-Break Moment.* Minneapolis: Carolrhoda Books, 2013. Read about the dangers and expanding science of head injuries in high school, college, and pro football.

NFL
http://www.nfl.com
The official website of the NFL is the main source for current news, history, and statistics about the National Football League, home of the most elite football players in the world.

NFL. *NFL Record & Fact Book 2013 (Official National Football League Record and Fact Book).* New York: Time Home Entertainment, 2013. Look up all the stats and records from the 2013 NFL season.

Pro Football Reference
http://www.pro-football-reference.com
You'll find a vast collection of professional football statistics and data.

Savage, Jeff. *Tom Brady.* Minneapolis: Lerner Publications, 2015. Tom Brady is one of the most successful quarterbacks in NFL history. Read all about his life in this up-to-date edition.

Sports Illustrated Kids. *Sports Illustrated Kids Big Book of Who: Football.* New York: Time Home Entertainment, 2013. Check out profiles, facts, and stats about the best players in pro football history.

Stewart, Mark, and Mike Kennedy. *Touchdown: The Power and Precision of Football's Perfect Play.* Minneapolis: Millbrook Press, 2010. This book is chock-full of fascinating football stories, statistics, memorabilia, and much more.

Index